THE BROKEN RULES OF ENGAGEMENT

If you can mend your broken Lamp,
then it will shine again.

If not you'll have to sit in the dark...

When you mend something,
you fix it and make it better.

PINKY THOMPSON

The Broken Rules of Engagement

ISBN 978-0-620-80068-6

First published in South Africa in 2018 by Thompsonlit.

Email: thompsonlit101@gmail.com

Phone: 084 419 8895

ACKNOWLEDGEMENTS

I thank God, the Almighty for the manifestation of His promises. I ask God to continue blessing me with wisdom, understanding and sound mind so that I can bless others through my tongue and not destroy.

To my husband Calvin, your tender love ignites and unleashes the best in me...always. Thank you for believing in me and encouraging me to never feel intimidated by the gap between my dreams and reality.

To my son Tshireletso, my everlasting joy, thank you for your "clever brains". Each time I study or write books, you would fondly come to me to rub your forehead against mine saying that "Come Mama, I'm anointing you with my genius brains so that you can pass like me at school in Jesus name", and it worked hey! I love you boy…

Mrs Magdelina Selepe my mom, who is my mentor too passed unto me her attributes of resilience, taking the pain and build something out of nothing. I celebrate your life "Mankele". My first love…

To the exceptional leaders who mentored me from a distance, I will forever be indebted to you, for your leadership, guidance and for leading me through your actions. The Almighty brought you into my life for a purpose to lead and transform me. This was achieved through your unreserved support.

I respect you, Mr HAN Jinghua: CEO of Palabora Mining Company as you truly lead by example and with great wisdom. You came to Phalaborwa with a driven purpose, and evidently, transformation and opportunities were realized by successfully creating shared value for all stake-holders. You are the Legend. May the good Lord protect you and your family. I salute you.

CONTENTS

PROLOGUE

The subject addressed in this book is complex and requires triangulations of approaches. Thus, it cannot be addressed just in one book. This is the first of the trilogy on the subject and the second book will be published in due course.

The perspective given is based on tacit knowledge, discussions and experiences from my own life and I think sharing these experiences would assist many organizations to grow, make a profit, create employment and continue sustaining economies in their countries. Although this book gives a South African perspective, the subject addressed is universal and applicable to organizations in other countries.

INTRODUCTION

This is an overview of line management, and about how they manage their reporting staff and set the tone for the entire business operation. As you explore this book, it reveals to Top management what are these broken rules of engagement at the workplace and what happens when the enemy is within your camp. The danger is, "If you don't know it is there, you can't fix it."

Top management will further discover what is it that consumes and exploit their organizations' time, resources and profits, and has resulted in a substantial number of employees disengaged and emotionally disconnected from their organizations.

Distinctive research has confirmed that employees feel that Top management is turning a blind eye on human resources elements that have a negative bearing towards employees. The employees reckon that Top management plays a little role in determining what the root cause of this predicament is and prohibiting it from recurring. The truth of the matter is that Top management is overlooking the issue of managing and mobilizing people. Their focus is mainly on making profit, sales, production outputs, increasing revenue, and other external elements that can affect the profitability of their businesses like commodity prices, exchange rate volatility, fluctuating economic conditions, determining methods to improve the organizations' reputation or securing license to operate, whilst the enemy is operating from within, leaving employees feeling despondent, unmotivated and unproductive, hence high rate of staff turnover.

This matter destroys the employees' morale and imposes a significant impact on productions, safe work practices, quality of the products and services, distributions and sales, etc. Top management has a duty to intervene and take corrective actions on this dilemma before they could severely suffer irreversible consequences of disregarding their organizational internal human resources environment. Several organizations to date are counting millions of rand per year in lost productivity, losing clients due to the poor quality of their products and services, excessive absenteeism from work in general and other problems that result when employees are disengaged at work. The provocative question is what went wrong? Was it the strategic decisions or the strategy implementation that went wrong?

CHAPTER 1

~∞~

ORGANIZATIONAL INTERNAL ELEMENTS

An organizational internal environment is composed of the elements within the organization. The elements include current employees, management and especially corporate culture, which defines employees behaviour, etc. Some organizational internal elements have an impact only to the employees, whereas others can affect management and leadership only or the entire organization as a whole.

Misalignment of Organizational Internal Elements to the Organization' Strategy

It is evident that there is a misalignment of the organizations' objectives and goals somewhere during the formulation or implementation stages of the organizations' strategy. This emerges where you find that the organizational internal elements do not support the organizations' strategy. As a result, the strategy will not meet its objectives or serve the purpose intended. To date, organizations have implemented their strategies into action in order to accomplish the desired strategic objectives and goals. By this time of the year, Top management should be able to determine whether their organizations' strategy was effectively implemented or not.

Most organizations have implemented brilliant strategies however, at the same token, those brilliant strategies have failed easily, as plans are often simply agreed to and then forgotten about within a few months down the line. Organizations tend to lose momentum. Others cannot adapt and are resistant to change in the scope of work. Some organizations have forsaken their strategies completely. This has been seen occurring in most organizations that have no monthly or quarterly strategy meetings with established reporting or scorecard system to monitor and track progress and the plan.

Top management in most instances fails to foster leaders in their organizations that have a need and capabilities to drive for progress hence the failure of organizational strategies. Organizations can benefit from such leaders who possess capabilities to drive for progress, as they are able to identify, diagnose and offer remedy actions. They do not watch and wait until when something goes horribly wrong and start blaming one another.

Organizations need leaders who can evaluate and assess challenges by looking at the discrepancy between the current state and desired state. Compare current against past performance, and current performance to other organizations. Then from their findings, compile and draft realistic future expectations and a plan to fix the misalignment, utilize state of the art technology and continuous improvement, etc. It is advisable for organizations not to just fix or adjust the misalignment, but to eliminate it altogether.

Organizations need to understand and establish that why the strategy has failed or heading that way as the first step. The problem may actually be an opportunity that needs to be exploited or a gap between what the organization is doing now and what it can do to create a more positive future. Assigning a task team and a good strategic plan will come in handy. It will assist and provide organizations with the roadmap they need to pursue a specific strategic direction, set of performance goals, deliver customer value, and be successful.

Continuous assessment and follow-up is essential and recommended to maintain a competitive advantage. Finally yet importantly, organizations need to adjust their operational strategy in response to significant internal and external opportunities and threats on regular basis.

Indications of an Out of control Organization

Slack Top management: Line management do not emphasize and value the need for controls, or they set a bad example.

Absence of policies and lack of agreed-upon standards:

It is where you find that the organization members are unclear about what needs to be achieved and the organization's expectations are not established in writing.

Shoot the messenger management: Employees feel their careers would be at risk if they report bad news (the truth).

Lack of ethics in the culture: Organization members have not internalized a commitment to integrity. Lack of periodic reviews: Managers do not assess performance on a regular timely basis.

Bad information systems: Key data is not measured in a timely and easily accessible way.

Evaluation of Organizational Internal Elements

It is very imperative that Top management should continuously evaluate their organizational internal elements. It will assist them to identify where they can implement more efficient techniques, to ensure that the organizational internal elements align with their organizations' strategy. Every Chief executive officer (CEO) or Managing director should know and be content that their organizations' structures, culture, mission, vision, IS&T, reward and recognition systems and leadership align with their organizations' strategy.

Does the culture reinforce and connect with the mission and vision of your organization? To be fully effective, the organizations' strategic, tactical and operational goals and plans consistent, mutually supportive and focused on achieving the common purpose and direction.

Strategic measurement can help in implementing the strategic plan. Appropriate measures show the strategy is important to the leaders, provide motivation, and allow for follow-through and sustained attention. As we go along this book, we will learn more about strategic measurement in details. They can increase the focus of the strategy, greater accountability since responsibilities are clarified by strategic measurement and better communication of responsibilities. Measures show what each group's primary responsibility is and which may reduce duplication of effort.

■ Organization Strategy's alignment to Vision & Mission statement

In general, organizations' strategies are geared towards realizing its vision by executing its mission and achieving its objectives. Mission and vision statements should be in place reflecting the mind, heart, soul, passion and resources of the organizations and stakeholders. In many organizations, statements are defined, but the question is, was the statements understood by all the employees as they are the key managers of the business in an essence? Is the statement consistently emphasized, by whom, on which platform and how frequent?

Through a strategy map, creating value by aligning goals is one method of aligning the organizations' strategic and operational goals. It is a tool management can use to communicate their strategic goals. It enables members of the organizations at every level to understand the role they will play in helping to achieve them.

What good is the mission statement if it does not describe who we are and what we do as an organization? The statement should differentiate the organization from its competitors, and recognizes its uniqueness and value to customers. The mission statement provides a statement describing the products, markets, corporate culture and overall financial goals of the organization.

In addition, organizations should continuously develop an understanding of customers' perspective and opinion of their organizations. Ask the question for example, how do the most profitable customers view the organization versus the views of the least profitable customers? How do the same customers view the key competitors? What products or product lines represent the greatest and least profit contribution and why?

■ Management and Leadership's alignment to Organization Strategy

High-performance organizations have aligned their management and leadership with their organizations' strategy. They strive to identify ways to improve or modify their leadership style and continuous leadership skills development. The Leadership philosophy or style varies from organization to organization and directly affects employees.

Most organizations prefer the democratic leadership style and obtaining input from subordinates when making decisions. Embarking on leadership that believes that there is no right or wrong decision yet forges business promoting decisions upon past, present and beliefs for the future. Leadership that does not have the answers yet knows the questions to ask and is willing to gain input from those closest and those furthest from the issue. Here we talk management and leadership's ability to communicate and conduct bottom-up strategy, as well as to make decisions consistent with the organizations' values.

Leadership must include strong ethical and morals values. Organizations need to strive to fall into the Leadership Grip (Fig 1.a below) that shows a high level of concern for employees while striving for a high level of concern for production namely great teamwork in the organizations. In grid training model, managers are rated on their performance-oriented behaviour (concern for people) and maintenance-oriented behaviour (concern for production). Preferably, the management style should be that of a transformational manager, motivating people to obtain their personal interest for the sake of the team and the organization.

Is your management and leadership style aligned with your organizations' strategy? Work on corrective measures you will need to apply to get them to support the vision, mission and goals of your organizations.

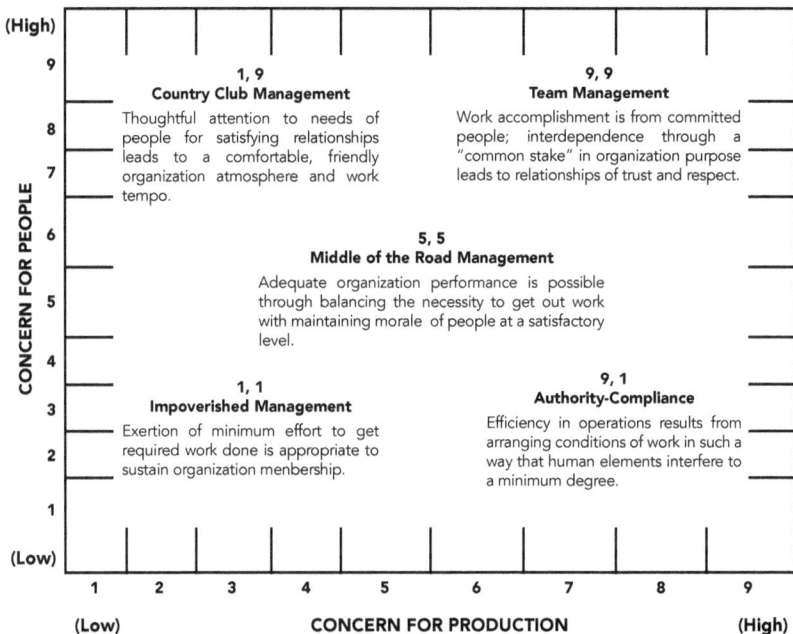

(High)

9

1, 9
Country Club Management
Thoughtful attention to needs of people for satisfying relationships leads to a comfortable, friendly organization atmosphere and work tempo.

9, 9
Team Management
Work accomplishment is from committed people; interdependence through a "common stake" in organization purpose leads to relationships of trust and respect.

5, 5
Middle of the Road Management
Adequate organization performance is possible through balancing the necessity to get out work with maintaining morale of people at a satisfactory level.

1, 1
Impoverished Management
Exertion of minimum effort to get required work done is appropriate to sustain organization menbership.

9, 1
Authority-Compliance
Efficiency in operations results from arranging conditions of work in such a way that human elements interfere to a minimum degree.

CONCERN FOR PEOPLE

(Low)

1 2 3 4 5 6 7 8 9

(Low)   **CONCERN FOR PRODUCTION**   **(High)**

Fig 1.a: Source: The Leadership Grip Figure from leadership Dilemmas-Grid Solutions, p 29, by Robert R, Blake and Anne Adams McCanse.

■ Organization Strategy's alignment to Organizational Culture

Individuals have personality and organizations have culture. The organizational cultures need to synchronize with the organizations' strategy. Management must also recognize the existing organizational culture and learn continuously to work within or change its parameters.

Organizations should instil the culture of entrepreneurship. Employees within the organizations are dynamic. They desire and wish to be entrepreneurial and are prepared to take risks as much as Top management are entrepreneurs and innovators who are willing to take risks. Values such as commitment to innovation and flexibility should prevail.

Strategic priorities must be geared toward growth and innovation. Organizations should reinforce a set of values and principles that create a consistent culture across their enterprise.

The culture should be motivating to employees and not be a toxic organizational culture where leaders are vindictive and do not create opportunities for employees to excel. Motivation and publicly celebrating large and small wins, such as the achievement of milestones will go a long way.

Through different thinking, management should foster creativity, encourage thinking outside of established boundaries and engage in informed risk-taking. They should trust in people, by being committed to attracting, engaging, developing and retaining the best people, while providing a great place to work with opportunities for continuous learning. Managerial, leadership and sales training are just a few of the programs in which our employees around the globe participate.

Management should encourage performance focus culture where everyone is committed to delivering top-tier results, relentlessly focus on planning, executing and exceeding expectations with accountability. The business processes used to manage the organizations and execute strategies for customers should include Lean and Six Sigma.

Leaders should have integrity, always. They must treat employees fairly, demonstrate trust and attempt to do the right thing always. Through an inclusive setting, certain organizations believe in individuality makes us collectively stronger.

In an essence, culture regulates the employees' behaviours and guides the action. It reduces the company uncertainty and provides a balance for all the staff.

■ Resources & Capabilities supporting the Organization Strategy

The organizational capability and resources should be well prepared to support strategy. Through the supportive and primary activities of the organizations, they are able to promote their primary goal of a superior product and service.

Do you have the ability to manage your resources, such as employees effectively to gain an advantage over competitors? The organizational capabilities should be unique to the organization to prevent replication by competitors and focuses on the business ability to meet customers demand. Capabilities that provide a competitive advantage include knowledge, product licenses and innovative designs.

The flexibility and responsiveness of the organization is its ability to change in response to customers' demand. The knowledgeable and skilled employees are organizational capabilities that provide organizations with the ability to respond to customers' demands and remain flexible to changes in the business environment. In addition, they will allow the organizations to direct those skills to achieve the business goals. Training programs, education assistance and effective recruiting and hiring programs are organizational capabilities that ensure a knowledgeable workforce.

The relationship between the organizations and their customers is an organizational capability that affects sales, reputation and loyalty for future business. Improved good customer relationships will ensure the continued growth and competitiveness in the market. Maintaining existing relationships with customers as well as developing new ones ensures the organizations will grow and thrive in the future.

The question to ask is "Are there enough resources to invest in areas of critical need?"

■ Strategy Control Systems

The tools used as the strategy control system should be effective and support the strategy implemented. There are various tests for organizations to conduct and can choose from in order to ensure that their strategy is winning and is on the right track. The tests range from the strategic fit test, competitive advantage test and performance test to evaluate and control.

Strategic thrusts will provide information that helps determine whether the overall strategy is shaping up as planned. With milestone reviews, organizations will be able to monitor the progress of the strategy at various intervals or milestones. This can be done carried out on a quarterly basis and be presented for approval varying from organization to organization is reporting structures like audit and risk committees and board meetings, etc.

The strategic processes should be effective and help to guide management to determine what to control, set control standards, measure performance, compare the performance to the standards, determine the reasons for the deviations and take corrective action to obtain desired outputs. The control systems include feedback of control information to the individual or group performing the controlled activity. Strategic audit measurement methods like qualitative organizational measurement need to be applied.

Review of performance should be conducted annually to see how the business is performing against any risks affecting the business and what they should do to mitigate the risks in future and improve performance. Risks can be market risks, technology competition, government tariffs and customs duties and increased raw material prices, etc.

What Organizations needs to do to achieve Strategic Goals & Objectives

The organizations' products and services need to be objectively and effectively matched to the market segments. This will help to focus the strategic planning activities of the organizations in areas of highest volume potential and highest financial return. Organizations must have a business plan that contains a list of key success factors. These are indicators or milestones that measure their business achievements and help determine how well they are progressing towards their goals and objectives. Key opportunity success factors are defined by the market and by the customers, not by the organizations. They revolve around skills, processes and systems.

Marketing and sales constraints, legal and political constraints, environmental constraints, logistical constraints and social constraints are the constraints or risks organizations need to overcome. There are also the factors that will make this the right choice.

Skills and human resources, capital requirements, market development, partnerships and stakeholder management are the critical success factors that need to be true for realizing the opportunity.

Creating Shared value

Creating shared value (CSV) for all stakeholders, that is what organizations need to focus on in order to manage the risks associated with the execution of its strategy. The competitiveness and the health of communities around the organizations are closely intertwined. A business needs a successful community to provide demand for its products and to supply critical resources for its operations. Organizations are often perceived to make profits at the expense of society, this perception is a threat to sustainability.

Unlike corporate social responsibility (CSR), creating shared value initiatives are not about making the trade-offs, as they seek to improve business profitability while providing social benefits. Rather than redistribute company's wealth (as in CSR), CSV seeks to create more wealth for all stakeholders. The value of such initiatives considers both costs and benefits. CSV is about generating new value for the business and its focus is on supporting communities in ways that improve business performance.

CHAPTER 2

◈

IDENTIFYING THE ENEMY WITHIN

The enemy operating within the organizations in this context can be anything ranging from deficiencies, deviations, variations, defects, waste, malfunctions, inefficiently utilization of company's resources, alienation and undervalue of employees by Line management and lack of ethical leadership, etc. In order for Top management to identify the enemy within, they need to strategize, as a ploy to outsmart the enemy.

Radical disruption of the Enemy's Programme

Sooner than later, Top management needs to get directly involved in their business dealings, especially at an operational level and refrain from relying entirely on Line management's reports. Top management can be able to achieve this by analysing their organizational internal human resources environment and analysing their operational internal controls. Organizations can also attain this through conducting bottom-up approaches. Getting to know and interacting with the employees at the operational levels should be a starting point. This will aid Top management to perceive and comprehend dynamics from their employees at the operational levels' point of view, and that, its the only way Top management can infer the enemy's true intentions. By so doing they can be able to detect the discrepancies and deviations, execute their response plan and then develop a solution appropriate to the analysis.

Disregarding employees at operational levels has landed many CEOs and their executives in hot water, some are facing legal battles whereas on the other hand others are shutting down their businesses. Line management has a tendency of hiding crucial information from Top management. They only report what Top management would like to hear until the inevitable happens. Employees at operational levels are instructed not to say anything to anyone concerning their working conditions. They've been warned and classically conditioned never to report deficiencies and deviations to the "big bosses". Employees are afraid of being alienated or victimized and worse their jobs are being threatened constantly!

Identify Chickens that eat their own Eggs

Companies CEOs, as a matter of urgency, should identify and address Line management and employees who exploit their own companies' resources, outputs and profit (chickens that eat their own eggs). This behaviour reflects a lack of discipline and lack of ethics as employees fail to maintain what they have acquired and achieved through hard labour. Employees in general work hard for their companies. They reach targets, productions are very high, sales are booming and without a doubt, it is expected for companies to make profits. However, some companies' income statement is in the red! What is the root cause?

Its time now for companies CEOs to meet the enemy within, wearing power suits, a smooth operator with cruel intentions, attending the same meetings with you, formulating organizational strategies and drawing company budgets with you.

In various organizations, exploiting the company's resources and money started as a mistake. Employees would accept small bribes, accidentally or intentionally double paying suppliers, over or under budgeting deficiencies, and making misconstrued mistakes. The day they have discovered and realized that its feasible easy money, undetectable and that they can actually get away with murder. It was too late for their companies CEOs before they knew it, their companies were suffocating in debts already and could do with some serious cash flow injections. This behaviour can spread quickly amongst other employees if left uncorrected, and it can be difficult to stop. Breaking this habit will require the companies CEOs to do everything in their power to identify and remove the egg-eating chicken (s) as soon as possible. You may not be able to catch the perpetrator in the act, but if rigorous audits and investigations of the employees is conducted, you should be able to detect who is responsible.

This book will teach you how to effectively analyse your organizational internal human resources environment and operational internal controls. It will further provide guiding principles on how to work and act quickly to stop this unacceptable behaviour before it affects the entire workforce. Bear in mind that when an employee consistently engages in undertakings and behaviours that contradict the desired and required conducts of an organization, this affects their personal performance as well as the performance of the organization.

Analysing Organizational Internal Human Resources Environment

The internal environment of human resources management (HRM) consists of unions, organizational culture, conflict, professional bodies, organizational objectives and policies, etc.

To be able to identify the enemy within the organizations, Top management should first analyse their organizational internal human resources environment, do some introspection. Do we know our business, what does the day-to-day running of the organizations we manage entails? Do we know our employees, the very ones at operational levels? What their needs are and their limitations? Do we value their inputs? Do we know what they think of the Management and leadership style? Whom do they turn to at times where there are loggerheads between themselves and Line management? Is our organizations' internal support structure for our employees effective enough to mediate? Does it resolve matters and prevent internal avoidable issues that could result into the resignation of highly valued employees with prominent talents and skills?

The organizations' management that would honestly don't just merely answer the above questions, but put them into perspective, review their internal processes, policies and procedures, conduct rigorous evaluations, interventions, call for radical change and forges proper governance structures to effectively implement their HRM strategic plan. Those organizations will definitely succeed and will reap benefits for both Top management and their employees as a whole. Most importantly, whatever deviations, deficiencies, malfunctions, employees' alienation by Line management and lack of ethical leadership would be uncovered and remedial actions can be enforced. Top management will have to come up with the overall plan that leads the implementation of specific HRM functional goals. HRM strategies guide personnel decisions that ensure the best fit for the organizations and all functional areas of HRM strategies need to match the overall business strategy.

Through Bottom-up Approach

To achieve the desired outcome, Top management should involve teams at all levels (operations) in strategic planning. This will help to build a shared vision and increases each individual's motivation to see plans succeed as opposed to Top-down strategy. Top management reaps good benefits when they involve employees in decision-making processes. It motivates them and they become more committed. Engaged employees increase production output and make a profit for their organizations. They achieve the business outcomes of their roles.

Successful organizations are driven by the operation principle "from implementing - to supporting - to driving strategy." Operational definitions should not be overlooked. Each functional area should create their own definitions to ensure agreement and commitment. To be fully effective, the organizations' strategic, tactical and operational goals and plans must be aligned, that they must be consistent, mutually supportive and focused on achieving the common purpose and direction.

Getting to know your employees

Open door policy/open to employee suggestions, you need to be familiar with your Line management's teams, interact and get to know them. However, on the other hand, you do not want to undermine their authority. Any interactions should be above board with the explicit goal of trying to better understand the team and help the manager. Do not allow yourself to get into the situation where you are hearing issues that they are not telling their manager. Be clear with everybody that you are aligned and there are no secrets. However, do not close off all communication.

There should be an effective implementation of a proper controlled platform like bossbarad, where employees can interact directly with Top management, for instance every semester to raise both their concerns. To ensure that the vision is shared, teams need to know that they can test the theory, voice opinions, challenge premises, and suggest alternatives without fear of being reprimanded.

Analysing Operational Internal Controls

Are your operational internal controls tightened? Only CEOs that demonstrate the strong support for internal controls by getting directly involved to establish and guide integrated internal control framework will be content to answer this question to their board directors.

Internal control is a process for assuring the achievement of an organization's objectives in operational effectiveness and efficiency, reliable financial reporting and compliance with laws, regulations and policies.

Without adequate internal controls, management has little assurance that its goals and objectives will be achieved. Properly designed and functioning internal controls will assist organizations to ensure that divisions are performing as expected on a daily basis whilst significant errors, fraud and deficiencies can be detected sooner rather than late when everything been has left in the hands of finance for audits purposes.

News flash! External auditors are not responsible for an entity's internal controls. External auditors evaluate internal controls as part of their audit planning process, but they are not responsible for the design and effectiveness of your controls.

■ Segregation of duties

Segregation of duties is a key internal control intended to minimise the occurrence of errors or fraud by ensuring that no employee has the ability to both perpetrate and conceal errors or fraud in the normal course of their duties according to Penn Internal Audit.

Generally, the primary incompatible duties that need to be segregated are:

- Authorization or approval
- Custody of assets
- Recording transactions
- Reconciliation/Control Activity

Some examples of incompatible duties are:

- Authorizing a transaction, receiving and maintaining custody of the asset that resulted from the transaction.
- Receiving funds (checks or cash) and approving write-off of receivables.
- Reconciling bank statements/accounts and booking entries to general ledger.
- Depositing cash and reconciling bank statements.
- Approving time cards and having custody of paychecks.

If internal controls are to be effective, there should be an adequate division of responsibilities among those who perform accounting procedures or control activities and those who handle assets. Ideally, separate employees will perform each of the four major duties. In general, the flow of transaction processing and related activities should be designed so that the work of one individual is either independent of, or serves to check on, the work of another. Such arrangements reduce the risk of undetected error and limit opportunities to misappropriate assets or conceal intentional misstatements in the financial statements.

■ Monitoring signing authority protocol

There should be clear guidelines regarding the signing authority protocol Delegation of Authority (DOA) in every organization of which CEOs should be able to monitor and control. It is important that mitigating controls, such as a detailed regulatory review of the activities, be put in place to reduce risks.

As the CEO of the organization, one should be able to account for any incoming and outgoing funds that they have approved. Many organizations' CEOs lately hire and work independently with auditors to investigate every contract awarded and invoices amounting from R100 000.00 and above before committing their signatures for authorization. This is to guard against, hidden costs, shell organizations, mischaracterized expense, multiple reimbursements, overstated expense and any other deficiencies that can negatively affect their organizations from making profits.

■ Address Indirect related spend

Indirect and related spend take a massive share of total enterprise costs. This spending waste spans everything from marketing services, IT to travel, and capital equipment. Top management needs to manage this unaddressed spend as there is savings potential, e.g. flights and accommodations cancellation costs, etc.

Organizations need to look into innovative ways to minimize costs, cut-off excessive wastage and optimise with regards to this matter. Understanding where and why waste is happening in your business is the first step toward preventing and eliminating it, and a step closer to reclaiming a margin point or more in bottom-line value.

■ Mischaracterized expenses

Mischaracterized expenses include, mainly claim for items that don't seem to be business related. Claim for meals and entertainment when employees are not working, travelling or on weekends. Day in and day out organizations receive and process submission of false invoices with personal purchases on the organizations' credit cards or other organizations accounts, receipts that include items or meals for children, or from establishments in the employee's neighbourhood.

■ Hidden costs

CEOs should be able to detect hidden costs on the invoices before signing off for their final authorizations. The invoices should be clear and have a detailed description of the products or services rendered for which the supplier or contractor is billing organizations. Top management should guard against signing off invoices where the description only read "miscellaneous", rather call in the Line manager and request for an explanation and a proper breakdown of those miscellaneous items. The revised invoices should be furnished once the "miscellaneous" have been satisfactorily justified.

■ Overstated expenses

Top management should query invoices where they suspect that the prices have been over inflated. As a precaution, it is advisable to request for quotations (RFQ) from other suppliers to compare prices.

Invoicing via Shell Organizations

Submission of false invoices is almost a second nature in many organizations. A dishonest employee uses a well established entity or shell organizations to bill his own division and authorize the invoice for payment of goods or services that were not rendered by that shell organizations. Most CEOs relies entirely on Line management and their judgement. Whatever the Line management has approved goes and CEOs do not question anything. To avoid signing invoices from ghost organizations for the services that were not rendered in your organizations. The invoices must be submitted with signed supporting documents such as timesheet, job card and delivery note, etc. This will serve as an acknowledgement and proof of delivery of services. Internal audit should be conducted to investigate if services were rendered in your organizations within the confinement of the set standard procedures.

■ Invoicing Via no accomplice Vendors

Pay-and-return schemes:

Employees intentionally mishandle payments that are owed to legitimate vendors. One way to do this is to purposely double-pay an invoice.

■ Identifying training needs

Is it justified for a division/line manager to release five people of his employee capacity to attend the same training programme? Whereas in an essence it would have been beneficial for one person to attend and in return, the incumbent can transfer skills learned to his co-workers at no cost. Top management should seek justification from Line management for such expenses bearing in mind that such unnecessary costs, e.g course fees, travelling and accommodation expenses, fuel reimbursements and subsistence allowances consume the organizations' profit in a way. Research has shown that most employees spend organizations' money on trips travelling far for matters that can be dealt with over the phone or emails.

Build learning into every project

Organizations spent a lot of money sending employees for various training. Line/project managers do it with good intentions. However, it defies the purpose and becomes a problem since at the end of every project, most leaders don't ever follow up to review whether learning has occurred or the skill was implemented or not.

Incorporate Best practices in Expense management

Good intentions cripple organizations sometimes. Know to what an extent are the powers you are giving away to Line management, especially where money is concerned? Be in the know of what you are authorizing for. In an essence. Top management should be wary of those invoices that are brought in for their attention until the very last minutes for their authorization, when it is almost cut off time for payments. That is where most discrepancies occur.

Fraud happens and it can happen no matter what accountants put in place to stop it. However, understanding exposure and incorporating best practices in expense management will reduce risk and give greater transparency to the reimbursement process, as well as organizations codes of conduct.

Analysing Safe work practices

The safety of employees in every organization should come first, following established health and safety policies and procedures. Employers must demonstrate their efforts for enhanced employees' safety while on duty. All employees are entitled to work in environments where risks to their health and safety are properly controlled.

Employers should provide and supervise that their employees are wearing the correct personal protective equipment (PPE), maintains and properly stores their PPE.

It should be compulsory for every employee to attend all the safety training and safety meetings that their employers offer. The safety representatives of every division must keep an attendance register and the Line management should monitor the attendance register.

Employers should ensure that no employee is allowed to operate any equipment or machinery unless they have been properly trained and possess a competency certificate. This will eliminate or prevent unnecessary accidents in the workplace.

It is important to continuously conduct inspections to check if employees are adhering to safe work practices, as it will assist to eliminate slips, trips and falls. Are your employees lifting safely and helping others to do the same? Be your brother's keeper! It is where an employee immediately notifies his co-workers, supervisors of any identified damaged equipment, hazardous conditions or unsafe behaviour. Employees should be educated to label all the chemical containers and become familiar with material safety data sheets.

Employers should encourage their employees to speak and raise any concerns in relations to safety issues. It is very imperative that employees give suggestions to their employers to make processes safer. In other organizations, employees feel discouraged and see reporting of hazards to their superiors pointless as their input or suggestions are not taken into consideration and this put their lives in danger. Organizations should strive to ensure that they build a strong safety culture or pay the price. It doesn't have to be by the blood, sweat and tears of their employees. It is every employee's responsibility to identify job hazards and take the appropriate precautions to protect themselves and others. Employees should exercise their legal right to refuse to perform unsafe duties at any given time.

It is hard to come to terms with the fact that many accidents that have occurred in the workplace could have been prevented. To make matters worse, the very same accidents still occur in the same manner from the very same organizations. It is advisable for organizations to review and implement safety management systems, re-train all relevant employees on all relevant procedures and standards.

Promptly reported injuries, illnesses and near misses to a supervisor should be logged into the risk register and organizations should come up with preventable measures. Employers, unions and health and safety committees should fix deviations, conduct a comprehensive audit for similar deviations, investigate reasons for system failures and establish an action plan to prevent further recurrences of system failures.

Safety representatives should ensure that all employees are aware of the evacuation procedures and the location of emergency equipment. It remains the organizations' duty to fulfil its duty to create a conducive and safe working environment.

Housekeeping Inspections

The recent walkabout conducted in several organizations were not a pleasant sight at all and that did not reflect a good impression and a good mindset of their employees in general. There were papers flying all over, overgrown grass, lugger bins full to the brim, untidy workshops, no signage boards and blocked sewerage systems, etc. Maintaining personal work areas in a clean and orderly manner forms part of safe work practices.

Housekeeping is a huge concern. Top management needs to assign task teams to formulate monthly clean-up groups operation. Thereafter management must ensure that this standard is maintained throughout and it is auditable internally. Cleaning operations should also be further extended to the offices. Some offices, you might mistake them for a storeroom if not a workshop.

Assessing Security services

Can you account for what comes in and out of your business premises daily? In many organizations, there's a need to have security control mechanisms over their internal security services in order for them to prevent rapid escalation of theft that is unaccountable by neither their employees nor security personnel. Crime intelligence is the way to go, using advanced security technologies like spyware camera, recording devices and an alarm system.

CHAPTER 3

❧

REINFORCE AND CALL IN SPECIAL FORCES

Top management needs to establish core values. The core values, mission and vision elements, defines what an organization believe in, stand for and values more than profits, where the organization is going, and why the organization exists.

Organizations that succeed are the ones that reinforce these values every day through training sessions and find effective ways to integrate them into the organizations' operations. Organizational leaders need to enforce a high-performance culture and develop a culture of team-work. Leaders should endeavour to mentor their subordinates in order to encourage and better them to continuously improve their skills and work smarter.

Top management to Lead by Example

It should start right at the Top. Top management should lead Line management by example, in such a way that they would expect them to manage their own teams. Top management is expected that they should exhibit the right behaviour and business ethical values as Line management are watching and paying attention to their actions all the time.

Top management to help Line management to succeed

It is very important and beneficial to the organizations for Top management to intervene and help Line management to succeed. The approach should be, how could we help you? Most CEOs relies only on productions, finance, or safety month-end updates reported in their monthly meetings.

It's very rare where you would find the CEO of an organization in an informal session with a specific Line manager trying to understand for their own benefit what kind of challenges he/she is facing and what are his/her limitations. Asking how can he/she support them and try to come up with possible solutions or call in cross-functional teams to join forces on how to tackle this challenge together. This session should start with identifying the constraints and limitations.

■ Constraints

Attitudes constraint is one of the major contributions as it brings lack of corporation from some other functional departments into play. This negatively decreases productivity not to mention lowering the morale of the production/sales teams. Some constraints if not managed properly by Top management might leave the company bleeding and its employees disengaged and feeling very despondent.

Morale Constraint is caused by the lack of support for the project/production managers from the steering committees, project teams or tender adjudication committees, be it financially or commissioning.

Skills constraint affect production/projects because the project team lacks experience or skills to execute a project of a specific nature. Skills transfer becomes a problem when drastic jobs restructuring takes place, especially where some project team members are removed from the project without their line managers' concern.

Availability Constraints have to do with everything with regards to time management. Relevant stakeholders do not adhere to the agenda items, meetings commence late, others do not attend the meetings at all and as a result, the objectives of the meetings ended up not met.

Technical Constraints due to the lack of implementation and application of the latest state of the art technology that would provide new fast services, accurately and in high volumes to production purposes or customers.

Feasibility constraint: A Feasibility study is not properly conducted and in most cases, it is based on assumptions without basis. The needs of the targeted market on how they would prefer the products or services are not established and organizations end up with a high volume of produced products and there is no demand for it.

Risk assessment Constraint: No identification of the threats and risks associated with the new implementation of the project plan until something happens and the production has to be stopped.

■ Risk Management

Organizations should know how risk management or any other changes in the project or production processes should be controlled. Project management teams often use the statement of work (SWO) or project charter to establish risk limits (Larson & Gray, 2011). To manage risks more effectively the project manager should undertake the risk management process.

This process includes four steps; these are (Larson & Gray, 2011):

- Risk Identification
- Risk Assessment
- Risk Response Development
- Risk Response Control

If the project managers diligently follow these steps, organizations would be in a far better position to identify all the risk involved with the project and develop the appropriate corrective measures for them.

■ Management of change (MOC)

Management of change (MOC) is not effectively implemented or at least on time. Top management needs to implement change management methodology as it allows project managers to deal with both planned and unplanned changes effectively by involving the project team and stakeholders. This will assist them to review the changes accordingly in the project scope. Threats imposed by the change will be identified, analysed, and implement control measures prior to recommencing the new project.

Top management to manage Managers

Line management and how they manage their reporting staff set the tone for the entire business operation. Line management is the front line representation of the business. They are the mechanisms that hold your organizations together because all of your employees report to them for better or worst. The majority of communication about the business is channelled through Line management.

Too much power kills they say and too much power has been vested in the hands of the Line management. The time is now that the Top management should get involved in managing their Line management. Enforcing these will ensure that Line managers are producing good work as with any employee and that they effectively offer the support needed to their teams.

Line management cannot afford to set double standards. They should adhere to the same rules they ask their employees to obey. This has been seen in too many instances where managers' report on duty under the influence of alcohol or reporting late for work. This is the easiest and needless way to undermine your own authority.

Managing managers start with aligning your goals with theirs, providing feedback, and help them advance their careers.

Most organizations are into cost saving initiatives. They have cut down on career development, which is one of the important element. This will always remain primarily one of the frequent arguments against investing in professional development: "what happens if organizations train their people and they leave?" A provocative question is "what happens if you don't train them and they stay?" When you have talented employees, it's up to you to keep finding areas in which they can improve to expand their skill set.

Managing Line management also requires leadership coaching, you have to coach managers to develop the culture and capabilities that their team members need. Teach the values through orientations/training sessions.

Top management should develop an effective apprenticeship model where they would train, explain, show their Line management what is expected from them and offer support where is needed especially during the conceptual stages. As time goes, Top management should make time to do things like participating in team meetings with their line management and observe them give feedback to their subordinates. Occasionally they can do the real work together with them or plant walkabouts as opposed to micromanaging. Whenever you are observing them, give immediate feedback as long as it is not in front of others in a way that undermines them.

Top management should occasionally shift focus on the specifics of Line management's work and discover their relationships with their subordinates, for example, you might ask the line manager, how's that project going? How are you working with Paul to get that project done? Alternatively, how might you better support John on that project by so doing, you talk directly about how they are coaching and giving feedback. This will serve as an indicator or a gesture to them that these things (projects) are important.

Complimenting Line management in public whilst their subordinates are watching will show that you value your reporting teams. Praise them publicly, ask for their advice in front of others, or assign them part of a presentation that lets them show off their expertise. Line management will be encouraged and do the same to their teams as well.

Provide operational autonomy. You don't have to necessarily dictate exactly how your Line management should do their job. Instead, give them advice and let them find their own authentic style. Every employee represents the brand. Every employee is accountable to the values, mission, and vision of their organizations as they represent the company. Values lose their credibility when leadership talks the talk but doesn't walk the walk, and when they lose sight of what the values mean to both the employees and customers experience. Leaders can avoid this outcome by remaining committed and intentional in building a values-centric culture.

CHAPTER 4

❦

PEOPLE DON'T LEAVE JOBS, THEY LEAVE MANAGERS!

Fear, avoidance, and high rate of staff turnover occur when employees think management is bad. When employees resign, the top reason for their resignation is their relationship with their manager. People leave managers, not jobs or employers, hence manage the manager initiative. It is whereby managers would be coached for success as that will be most beneficial to top management, employees and the organizations as a whole.

Many have lived to tell tales as they have seen high-powered careers obliterated and powerful organizations almost brought to their knees by reckless leadership behaviour. All of these unwelcoming behaviours are unacceptable at work, yet they occur daily in the workplaces worldwide.

■ Poor Managing People Skills

Notably, many Line managers lack fundamental training in managing people. They lack the right attitude of work and life. Most importantly, they lack the values, empathy, and the capability that is required to interact effectively with their employees in the workplace.

It is easier to teach skills and techniques, but values, beliefs, and attitudes are much harder to teach and harder for managers to learn. Yet, these are the most underlying issues that will make managers successful or not.

Top management in people-oriented, forward-looking organizations, before thinking about assessing people for a job, they have to pass through three screens (acid tests) namely the test for integrity and attitude, intelligence and maturity.

Top management need to assure their success in managing people by selecting the right line management. They need to select people with passion who really care about colleagues and employees winning. Cultural fit should be considered along with job competencies when making hiring decisions for managers. Within the cultural fit component of your interview and selection process, a candidate for a managerial position must demonstrate that he or she has beliefs, values, and a work style that are congruent with those of your organizations. This includes having a commitment and a desire as a candidate for a managerial position to create an environment that empowers and enables employees to continuously grow and contribute to their success.

Characteristics to look for when interviewing and Selecting Line managers

- Effective communication and listening skills
- Value people.
- Integrity
- Business ethics
- Accountability
- Reliability and Dependability
- Believe in empowering and developing employees
- Demonstrate leadership and the ability to set a clear direction.
- Believe in teamwork
- Place the customer at the centre of their reason for existence and regard reporting staff as customers

■ Emotional Intelligence

In the workplace, most of you came across far too many occurrences of managers throwing objects, yelling, making people cry, and other tell-tales signs of an emotional hijacking. Employees dread going to work because of such behaviours. As the manager, you can't afford to break down when the pressure is on. The ability to remain calm accepts the situation and then focuses on a solution is essential in a good manager. An emotional hijacking demonstrates low emotional intelligence and it's an easy way to get fired. As soon as you display that level of instability, employees will question whether you're trustworthy and capable of keeping it together when it counts. Screaming at people, irrespective of how much they might "deserve it", turns a huge amount of negative attention your way. You'll be labelled as unstable, unapproachable, and intimidating.

Controlling your emotions keeps you in the driver's seat. When you are able to control your emotions around someone who wrongs you, they end up looking worse instead of you. In reality, the problem is not actually the problem; the problem is the way one responds to the problem. It is strongly recommended that Top management should provide 360° feedback and executive coaching.

■ The Insecure Manager

Managers are supposed to motivate employees, not compete with them. Yet, many supervisors impede talented employees and good ideas because of their own insecurities. These managers are insensitive and self-doubting managers. They fear the unknown and assume the unintended. Some Line managers will constantly badmouth high-performing employees whom they suspect, are very close to their boss. One will never grow and be developed under such toxic and tyrants leadership, hence resignation of highly valued employees with prominent talents and skills. They do everything in their power to jeopardize and sabotage every opportunity for their subordinates to grow within the company.

■ Lack of Respect

Line management and their reporting teams, they do not have to like each other. However, they are compelled to work together in harmony and respect for each other to support the vision and mission of the employer. At all costs, leaders should never yell or raise their voice to the reporting staff. This shows a lack of respect for them. Line managers should shy away from criticizing employees in front of their peers. It is good workplace manners to call them aside and point out to them privately where they did wrong. Employees know when they are not respected and they will hate you. When you ignore their inputs, and criticize them unfairly and demonstrate a lack of respect, you injure their feelings, their self-confidence, and their self-esteem.

Let employees know that you care about them. However, make them realise everyone has a job to do, and that you are accountable to your boss, just as they are accountable to you. Line manager should be trained to treat employees with respect in order to increase productivity and engaged workforce.

"If you want your dinner, don't insult the cook."

■ Bully Managers

They are here, smiling and being friendly to others yet yells and curse at their reporting teams. They physically intimidate employees by physical proximity. They go to such an extent that they would block employees from getting away either from their desk or from the office. They treat employees at the workplace like school children, it's despicable. The sad part is, they know exactly what they are doing, they even plan for it and how it should affect the other person. You can even see that they get a kick out of doing that as they would even mention it to whoever cares to listen to what they did and how the victim reacted.

Bully managers intimidate employees with words, threaten employees and their jobs, and have even been known to throw objects at employees. They pull ranks whenever their subordinates try to raise issues concerning the business operations. They would say something like "you are way below my level. I can't have this conversation with you." If you are lucky to engage in a conversation with them, you must only listen to them telling you what to do. Your opinion is not acceptable as it is seen as one challenging them or refers to it as insubordinations. Bullies belittle employees and chip away at an employee's self-confidence and self-esteem with criticism, name-calling, and ridicule. Bullies are condescending, demeaning, and cruel. Poor employees are getting pushed out of their jobs and no one can save them from this power-driven managers.

Amongst other things that employees do question concerning the leadership styles. Two things can happen, subconsciously, employees make a decision to learn from their managers' leadership style on either "to learn how to become a good leader or learn how not to become a bad leader."

■ Promote and Hire the wrong people

It's sad how Line managers overwork employees with certain talent and skills in the workplace and even goes as far as committing to promote them and end up not honouring their commitments.

Employees will do their best to keep their managers pleased even if it kills them, taking away their time with their loved ones. Line managers will fail to acknowledge that and even take credit for their hard work. To make matters worse, unexpectedly, they even promote someone who is incompetent and less committed when it comes to their job. As if, it wasn't bad enough. Some of the tasks that they cannot execute, Line managers would assign them to the most hardworking employees to complete for them just because they are the Line managers' favourites.

Favouritism in the workplace is experienced every single day and has its negative effect on employees. Same applies to nepotism. Besides managers hiring inadequate candidates, they are also conflicted because they hire their immediate family members as well. That on its own is a major demotivating factor for those stuck working alongside them.

CHAPTER 5

AVOIDABLE BLUNDERS BY LINE MANAGEMENT

The sad thing is that these blunders by Line management can easily be avoided. All that is needed is a new perspective and some extra effort on the manager's part. It has nothing to do with ability, but with judgment and self-discipline.

■ Staff turnover

Staff turnover is the ratio of the number of employees that leave an organization through attrition, dismissal, or resignation during a period to the number of employees on payroll during the same period.

This shouldn't come as a surprise when you come across organizations that have on their payroll the "High-performance employees", the reason behind is, they are highly satisfied with compensation, benefits, non-monetary recognition and show appreciation for contributions when appropriate. This goes a long way, as it can give an employee the sentimental value "My supervisor values my contributions."

■ Retain good and talented employees:

- Additional investment in training programs offered in each of the group organizations.

- Being recognized for staff member's effort on addition work done through various programs or prices.

- Good communication systems where individual work structure, position and expectations is discussed and understood.

- Aim to retain and attract key skills to foster stability and business excellence. Strive to meet employment and compensation equity targets. The focus should be to ensure that all employees are excited, self-motivated and committed to their organizations.

Reward and Recognition Systems:

Comply with a legal requirement to ensure that government legislation is followed in terms of the Basic conditions of employment act (BCEA). Benchmark your packages against the industry and ensure that they are in line with your business.

■ Turning a blind eye

Line management in most organizations fails to listen to their employees and fail to make employees feel that their opinions are valued. It has been seen in several organizations where failure to react to problems and issues that will soon fester if ignored, has resulted in irreversible damages that have costs organizations millions of rand.

It is advisable for Line management to take time to listen to their employees regarding their concerns and needs for performing their jobs. Employees want open-mindedness. When your employee approaches you with their concepts, you need to treat them with sensitivity and honesty. Deliberate various issues with each employee individually, such as conflicts they may have with you or other employees. Resolve conflicts right away by coming up with feasible solutions. Use a mediator or arbitrator, if necessary, to handle conflicts out of your control. Keep the conflicts from amplifying or causing resentment, which can hinder productivity. Employees have a fundamental human need for connection with Line management.

■ Personalize your Approach

Learn the key strengths of your employees with respect to knowledge, education and skills. Assign employees project tasks that they are naturally good at performing. Allow employees to set their own job goals or methods for completing assignments. Encourage your employees to make recommendations that may help increase your organizations' performance and productivity. Recommend training for employees who need it, as they may get frustrated if they have trouble, using certain software programs, for example.

■ Poor Communication

Employees in most instances accuse Line management of failing to communicate effectively and withhold important information. The objectives are easily achieved when good communications are applied.

A manager with strong communication skills is able to instruct as well as listening. Managers who can communicate effectively can process information and then relate it back to their teams clearly. Effective managers should be able to understand, interpret, and relate the organizations' vision back to their employees in order to maintain productivity.

Good communications also help to solve complicated structures of the organizations. Electronic communication technologies are the most effective way to communicate and solve problems between different regions and departments.

Culture has an important role in communication for the organizations. It regulates the employees' behaviours and guides the action. It reduces the organizations' uncertainty and provides a balance for all the staff. Group meetings allow the employees to express their opinions that assist the group to continue to improve their flexibility and profits.

Failure to provide clear directions is another hindrance. Communicate with your employees on a regular basis. Keep them informed of the latest updates and encourage them to keep you apprised of their progress on certain projects. Ensuring clarity and consistent communication, from mapping desired outcomes to designing performance measures, seem to be essential to success.

■ **Lack of Employee Empowerment & Career Development**

There is a lack of developing the skills of more ambitious employees. Management does not offer programs that enable their team to continuously grow and contribute to their success.

The best managers know when their employees need development and how to ensure that those developmental opportunities are successful. Developing others involves cultivating each individual's talents and motivating them to channel their talents towards productivity.

Find out what drives and motivates each employee to perform at a higher level. Assign more tasks that are challenging and projects to those employees who want greater responsibilities. Empower employees to make their own judgments and decisions on certain projects. Tolerance of respectfully and professionally expressed differences of opinion is a key element of a healthy corporate culture.

Total Quality Human Resource Management

Alignment and cohesion in employees work could be achieved if they know and understand the nature of the business, shareholders, target market, customers' demands and needs. Well-defined standard operating procedures and policies help employees in achieving tasks and goals. Authority and autonomy should be given to employees in order to meet quality in the work. Employees should be shared important business news and their suggestions are welcomed if appropriate and relevant. Competencies and capabilities of employees should be enhanced through adequate training programs and development opportunities. Retention and commitment of employees are useful for uniformity and regularity in organizations operations. This would be gained by rewards and acknowledgement of employees work.

CHAPTER 6

❦

LEADERSHIP

Leadership involves focusing on producing change by developing a vision for the future along with strategies for bringing about the changes needed to achieve that vision. It is about aligning people by communicating the new direction, creating coalitions that understand the vision and are committed to its achievement.

Good leaders use motivation to energize people, not by pushing them in the right direction as control mechanisms do, but by satisfying basic human needs for achievement, a sense of belonging, recognition, self-esteem, a feeling of control over one's life and the ability to live up to one's ideals.

John Adair (1973) listed the following qualities that good leaders possess:

Enthusiasm - To get things done which they can communicate to other people.

Confidence - Belief in themselves, which again people can sense (but this must not be overconfidence, which leads to arrogance).

Toughness - Resilient, tenacious and demanding high standards, seeking respect but not necessarily popularity.

Integrity - Being true to oneself, personal wholeness, soundness and honesty, which inspire trust. Warmth in personal relationships, caring for people and being considerate

Humility - Willingness to listen and take the blame, not being arrogant and overbearing.

Lack of Ethical Leadership

Ethics relate to some rules, policies, norms, values and principles both individual and collective that guide actions to be taken in running an organization.

Line management in some instances engages in decisions that have resulted to a lack of trust in the organizational leadership, and lack of commitment to organizational goals. Ethical leadership includes transactional leader behaviours such as setting ethical standards and holding followers accountable for ethical conduct.

Lack of ethical leadership has always been one of the main reasons why organizations are left financially crippled by alleged and proven deficits in ethical leadership. Leaders should avoid or openly declare a conflict of interest, build business relations on transparency and fairness and adhere to the code of business ethics and conduct.

A true leader will not conspire with others to defraud the public and take unethical risks that endanger the funds invested in their organization. A good leader set respective goals and is willing to hold on to these goals even in difficult times.

The following recommendations from the empirical literature are guidance for corporate leaders in the management of ethical issues (Collins, 2010, Trevino & Brown, 2004, Upadhyay & Singh, 2010)

- **The CEO must be the chief ethics officer of his/her Organization.** This is necessary in order to personally assess areas for ethical risks such as guidance on ethical issues, monitoring the organization's adherence to ethical codes, monitoring an organization's ethics policy and overseeing ethics training programmes.

- **CEO he/she must ensure a strong ethical culture (a total quality management of ethics) within the workplace.** The values and norms of the workplace should be in accordance with set ethical issues complying with the systematic approach of total quality management of ethics. The total quality management approach to ethics can help to determine the root causes of ethical behaviour and be managed appropriately.

- **Organizations should strive to hire ethical people.** Organizations should focus on ethical skills along with the technical skills in the recruitment screening process. Information on potential employee ethical behaviour can be obtained from resumes, reference checks, background checks and integrity test.

- **Organizations should ensure that all employees participate in ethics training programmes.** This will serve as an opportunity for employees to learn and evaluate the impact of ethics on activities and organizational performance.

- **Corporate leaders should reward ethical conduct and discipline unethical conducts.** Leaders should make decisions that promote and compensate employees who are not only good on what they do but also have a sound relationship and have developed a reputation with customers and co-workers. The 360-degree performance management system evaluation can be used for ethical behaviour decisions.

"Be the master of your will and the
slave of your conscience."

Accountability

A true leader faces the music, even when he doesn't like the tune. Top management needs to instil or reinforce the trait of accountability in their Line management.

Being a good leader comes with acceptance of responsibility and liability for the outcomes expected of them both good and bad without shifting the blame to others or the external environment. Imagine a Line manager standing before Top management, other Line managers and the operational teams to address production loss during a meeting. Instead of accounting for it, worst of all, he blames it on his reporting staff. One will agree that this is not the kind of feedback Top management expected and needed to hear. The best approach would be to report to them, what is your plan, your strategy response plan, recovery plan, etc. An accountable manager will state how he is going to prevent this from occurring again.

A good manager will own the problem, once you own it, you can begin fixing it. Everyone is expected to take accountability for his or her work performance in the workplace. This eliminates a lot of wasted effort in playing the victim and blaming others.

The Danger of One side of the Story

Line management has a tendency to blame or misconstrue their subordinates to Top management for the discrepancies and mistakes that they have committed themselves. Unfortunately, this can be career limiting for their subordinates. In most instances, subordinates are being coated to be seen and labelled as incompetent in the eyes of Top management. The sad part is that: subordinates never get to hear about the vicious accusations against them and are not given an opportunity to defend themselves. If it happens that they tell their side of the story, poor subordinates will definitely, without a doubt, stand a good chance of being victimized.

According to Chimamanda Ngozi Adichie the single story creates stereotypes, and the problem with stereotypes is not that they are untrue, but that they are incomplete. They make one story become the only story. The consequence of the single story is this: It robs people of dignity. It makes our recognition of our equal humanity difficult. It emphasizes how we are different rather than how we are similar".

CHAPTER 7

❦

BOTTLENECKS

A bottleneck is a point of congestion in a production system that occurs when workloads arrive too quickly for the production process to handle. The inefficiencies brought about by the bottleneck often create delays and higher production costs.

In production and project management, a bottleneck is one process in a chain of processes, such that its limited capacity reduces the capacity of the whole chain. The result of having a bottleneck is stalled in production, supply overstock, pressure from customers and low employee morale.

Bottlenecks can cause major glitches in the organizations. Identifying their root causes is critical. Bottlenecks emerge in situations like where you find that job orders are generated, however, sit in one colleague's inbox or in-tray unprocessed for days because they are too busy or waiting to receive reports or pieces of information from another colleague but they are not liaising with them to expedite the process. These kinds of delays are unnecessary and hinder tasks and projects to be complete on the set dates. Reporting teams suffer the consequences, as they will be forced to wait unnecessarily for managers to release and authorize payments, purchase requisitions, purchase orders, etc. Many are guilty as charged. These display lack of support at times to reporting teams.

There are both short and long-term bottlenecks. Short-term bottlenecks are temporary and are not normally a significant problem.

■ Unblocking Bottlenecks

Identify bottlenecks such as backlogged work, if you are always late sending things to your colleagues and high stress relating to a task or process. To make sure you identify the root cause and not just one of the effects, use a flowchart or the five whys technique. Are there bottlenecks in any of your processes at work? For each bottleneck situation, identify who or what the bottleneck is. Is it you, or someone else, or even an automatic process? Then determine if the process would flow better if inputs to the bottleneck step were reduced or if efficiency were increased. If the problem is efficiency, how can you improve?

Delegation of Authority Inefficiency

The Delegation of Authority (DOA) is the formal process in which one person delegates the authority and responsibility to another person to carry out specific activities. However, the person who delegated the work remains accountable for the outcome of the delegated work.

DOA becomes a bottleneck take for instance it was found that in certain organizations, managers literally had the whole operations or specific projects placed on hold if not entirely jeopardized, whereby managers did not delegate any authority to subordinates during their absences and knowing very well that they will be out of reach for a good two weeks or so. Practically no one was assigned to act on his or her behalf to assume their signing and legal responsibilities. Organizations are losing millions of rand out of such act of recklessness. Poor subordinates are shown as incompetent and are blamed for projects failure, although the culprit is known and not being held accountable for anything.

If managers do not delegate when possible, they can become overloaded. Overloading causes vertical coordination to break down because the manager becomes a bottleneck rather than a facilitator. The leader that has to make every decision essentially becomes an authority hog, and they will never grow their organizations beyond their own decision-making capacity.

DOA should be done for developing others however, it becomes a bottleneck where a manager has placed his subordinate in charge, that particular individual is not properly trained, and not well familiar with the organization's policies that govern the authority delegated.

You should not delegate when:

- The task requires a skill-set or competency for which an employee is not qualified.
- The task do not runs parallel with the employee's career path.
- They are activities with poorly defined objectives.
- You don't have the time to set expectations, or support the employee along the way.
- You are not delegating for the right reasons, for example, giving work to someone only because you do not like to do it yourself, not that you are freeing yourself up to do something else.

Subordinates may not be developed to fill future managerial positions, thus weakening prospects for adequate vertical coordination in the future.

Lack of Succession Planning

What happens when the inevitable happens, when employees resign, retire, dismissed, get sick or pass away?

Due to this, a lack of succession planning can become a bottleneck.

The worst has happened! The division manager together with the HR manager of a certain organization in Durban knew for over 3 years that this specific employee is going to retire on a set date. Until the last date, there was no successor who was well trained for the position. Within 2 months upon retirement, the ex-employee was called back to come to help the employee who took over from them because he/she cannot perform certain crucial functions due to lack of adequate succession planning. Do you think for a minute that this proposition came at no costs? NO! Now the organization was faced with remunerating two employees for the same position whereas they could have trained the current employee for this role a long time ago with no expenses; whilst the ex-employee was still under their payroll.

It is a bottleneck for the organizations that bear negative consequences where underqualified employees are moving into roles and no efforts was made to identify and train high-potential workers to succeed in those key roles in future.

HR leaders must work to build strong cultures of learning that empower employees to cultivate the skills they will need in the future. Succession planning if it is well implemented and rolled out effectively, it will ensure that the business will continue to run efficiently. This can be realized by identifying and fostering high-potential workers through mentoring, training and stretch assignments for advancement into key roles.

By re-imagining learning strategies, organizations can better engage and empower employees to take control over their learning and career development. It takes courage to re-think once dependable processes and upend traditional learning approaches, but in order to grow and thrive, change is necessary.

Ineffective Management of Time

Most people fail to understand the concept of time, its value in life and other people whom with you interact. Managers should learn to manage their time effectively by so doing they would be exceptionally productive at work, and the stress levels will drop. Meetings are good, but one cannot spend most of the time in the boardrooms or lunchrooms as opposed to executing the actual tasks. What good is a meeting where no focus is given to the objective and task items assigned are not actioned? In most cases, meetings are not as efficient as should be to focus on high priority tasks.

Identified common time management mistakes:

- Procrastinating
- Failing to keep To Do List
- Holding unnecessary meetings
- Failing to set priorities
- Not delegating effectively.
- Failing to manage unwanted visitors or distractions
- Telephone interruptions

- Social chit-chats at work
- Travelling
- Dealing with other people's problems
- Not appreciating and understanding the concept

CHAPTER 8

∞

WHEN SILENCE IS NOT GOLDEN

In all the dynamics that we have emphasized and deliberated upon from Chapter 1, it clearly brings to light that there are many issues going on in the workplace that are not addressed or dealt with, at least at the right platforms.

Employees want transparency and little security. Employees need to know where the organization is going, whether the organization makes a profit or not. Employees want to know that they're not wasting their time when they're giving you their best. The best you can do is to help them to review their contributions.

If organizations constantly make employees feel insecure in their jobs, waver in their commitment to them, don't look after them and their best interests, and don't give them a future with their organizations, they will never achieve an engaged workforce, because true engagement is true commitment.

The communication channel between management and employees should always be open. Managers need to be able to talk about ordinary things with their employees before they can talk about anything major that will shatter their hopes.

When employees feel, they can't trust leadership they feel unsafe, like no one has their back, and then spend more energy on self-preservation and job hunting than performing at their job. Due to that, talent acquisition costs and employee turnover costs increase.

What employees need from employers?

Do you know the tangible and intangible important things that your employees need? It is not always about salary raise and bonuses. It is not a surprise that the most successful organizations are the ones that work the hardest to please their employees, and it's up to managers to make sure they are giving their employees what they need to the best of their abilities.

Daniel Pink's research:

Pink's research on what motivates employees has led him to one conclusion: "The best use of money as a motivator is to pay people enough to take the issue of money off the table." He says it's better to pay people a little more than the norm and allow them to focus on their work than to pay them based on performance. "Don't pay people a measly base salary and very high commissions and bonuses in hopes that the fear of not having enough food on their tables will inspire them to do extraordinary things."

Employees, in general, want to believe that their boss is a leader who is worthy of their loyalty and respect. They tend to respect a boss that will not generally say negative and offensive things. It kills the employees' morale when their managers do not have the time or the interest to hear them out of what they have to say. They just hate it when their managers dismiss their advice, they immediately assume that he or she does not care about them and their inputs are not valued. Gradually employees will switch to despondent and disengaged mode.

Employees want to be treated fairly in the workplace. They expect the perks and promotions to go to the employees who work hard, not over favouritism, nepotism and to people who are incompetent.

Employees want responsibility and to know that they are in control and can be trusted to execute their assigned tasks, and that makes them be more productive. They want to be coached not micromanaged. They will ask for help and intervention where and when there is a need. A little supervision and coaching here and there cannot hurt. What they hate is working under a manager who is constantly telling them what to do and witch-hunting.

Regardless of how employees are committed to their jobs, they do not like it when work keeps them away from their social life outside their work. It is shocking how Line management tends to forget and treat employees as if they don't have their own personal life.

Most Line management fails to plan work and they work their employees under pressure unnecessarily. Have you ever wondered why some employees do not give out their private contact numbers on their organizations' telephone directory? In addition, if they do, chances are it's a wrong number or resort to switching off their mobile phones. Employees need some time off from the workplace to rest.

In organizations, there is always too much to do and not enough time to do it and that leave employees feeling stressed and hopeless. Realistic goals are not set and on the other hand, managers expect the impossible outcomes from employees.

They overwork employees, rush them without giving out clear directions and eventually, they burn out and they crush. Most suffer from fatigues, etc. Managers need to set goals to be realistic, measurable and obtainable.

Employees are overworked and forced to perform extra duties that are not even in line with their organizations' role descriptions. The amount of time and energy consumed whilst performing such, shift their focus from their core organizations' role descriptions and they start to lag behind. The sad part is, when it comes down to the appraisals time, their managers only appraise them based on their key performance indicators (KPIs) and choose to forget the extra duties and not even appreciate what they have achieved outside their role KPIs. That is the broken rules of engagement in every sense of the word.

Employees appreciate working in an environment where they are allowed to foster innovation through employee brainstorming sessions that let the staff work with new people and generate fresh ideas.

CHAPTER 9

❧

DISENGAGED EMPLOYEES

No organization can afford to have disengaged employees. Disengaged employees don't have an emotional commitment to their work or their organizations and they have no intentions of helping it grow.

More efforts should be put in to raise levels and employees' morale of disengaged employees. They tend to feel their contributions are being overlooked, and their potential is not being acknowledged. They often feel this way because they don't have productive relationships with their managers or with their co-workers.

■ The Effect of Disengaged Employees

- ■ They do not take initiative, they want to be told what to do just so they can do it and say they have finished.

- ■ They act out their discontent and sow seeds of negativity at every opportunity. They express mistrust and outright resentment.

- ■ They are not just apathetic to the organizations goals and mission. They negatively influence or undermine the work of others.

- ■ Employees rely on each other to produce products and services. Excessive damage can be caused to the organizations' functioning due to tension fostered by disengaged employees.

- ■ They lie, gossip, and complain. Nothing is ever good enough for them, they make up stories, causes confusion around them and they never take responsibility for their actions and always find an excuse.

A good manager will identify those who are disengaged and explore the reasons behind the disconnect to determine if coaching or other interventions are appropriate

Managers need to demonstrate a sense of really caring about employees and what's important to them. Managers can help employees refocus on the demands of their roles and on the skills, knowledge, and talents they bring to their jobs. Engaging employees and keeping them engaged begins with asking them what they want and what is important in order to be effective in their roles.

The manager who takes the time to have a discussion about an employee's strengths and how these can make a difference forges essential ties and connections that lead to employee commitment.

■ The Power of Reciprocity shapes Engagement

What goes around comes around, and as engagement becomes more of a partnership, the power of reciprocity in the workplace takes shape. It's an unwritten social contract in the workplace "to attain commitment, we must commit to employees, to make employees care, we must care, to get employees to go above and beyond for us, so must we for them".

Experience the Power of Employees' Engagement

Leaders who encourage their employees to see how their work contributes to the organizations' future are the ones experiencing the power of employees' engagement. The objective is to focus employees on outcomes as well as the steps it takes to get there. Ask questions like, what are the outcomes (expectations) they are supposed to achieve? What were they hired to do? How do they contribute to making this a great place to work? Are they creating engaged customers?

Engaged employees, once assured have strong relationships and clear communications with their managers and being challenged in their areas of talent and strengths that is enough to stimulate them and ignites their potential and willingness to help the business grow. Provide employees with feedback and guidance regularly. There is no way to get better at something you only hear about once a year. Managers should help employees clarify how they can achieve outcomes.

■ Benefits of Engaged Employees

Engaged employees set goals, meet and exceed expectations and are enthusiastic toward the next challenging task. They have a clear path set for focusing on what they do best.

Engaged employees tend to be unlikely micromanaged because they deliver what is expected from them as they have clear communication channels with their managers. Engaged employees increase more productivity output, they generate profit for their organizations and they achieve the business outcomes of their roles. They produce products and services of high quality and drive customer engagement.

They contribute to good working environments where coworkers rely on each other and have a strong relationship with their manager. They feel a commitment with their coworkers enabling them to take risks and stretch for excellence.

They are more ethical and loyal to their managers. They are committed and contribute to the growth of their organizations.

Expectations, clarification and measurement are the keys to helping employees stay in the engaged range, and to keeping them involved and committed. Good measurement includes regular feedback, aligns with outcomes and matches the expectations for the role. Effective managers and leaders help their employees who work with them to design and own their own goals, targets and milestones. Great managers provide coaching to facilitate progress and build talents into strengths.

CHAPTER 10

❧

RULES OF ENGAGEMENT AT THE WORKPLACE

In the workplace, rules of engagement may refer to practices followed or appropriate behaviour displayed by both management and workers in the course of doing business. Engagement is a partnership between the organizations, leaders, and employees.

All businesses require competent employees in every position. Acceptance in the business is conditional, based on competence and the ability to produce and perform at a consistently high level. If a person is less than competent, they simply will not meet that standard.

To succeed, businesses must rethink how they engage, enable and earn the loyalty of their people. Engagement happens when the partnership is balanced and when everyone works together to make their work and the workplace more engaging.

■ Dependability and Reliability

Dependability and reliability in the workplace are easily recognizable traits, for instance being able to report to work on time, following through with assigned tasks, not abusing the organizations resources, power and being able and trusted to execute a given task without supervision. Dependability points to your personal integrity, which translates to respect, not only for your boss and co-workers but for yourself as well.

Employers want employees to be faithful and loyal to their cause, products, and organizations. However, will they give that same loyalty away? Employers must be completely committed and loyal to their employees if they want employees to be completely committed and loyal to them. These bring us to what obligations/duties does employees owe to their employer vice versa:

Obligations/duties do employees owe to their employer vice versa:

DUTIES OF EMPLOYER	DUTIES OF EMPLOYEE
• To accept the employee into his services.	• To make his personal services available.

DUTIES OF EMPLOYER	DUTIES OF EMPLOYEE
• To provide the employee with work. • To pay the agreed remuneration. • To pay a quantum merit. To provide safe working conditions. • To comply with statutory duties.	• To warrant his competence and reasonable efficiency. • To obey the employer. To be subordinate to the employer. • To maintain bona fides. • To exercise reasonable care when using the employer's property. • To refrain from misconduct.

Furthermore, employees are expected by their employers to do what a reasonable employee would do in any situation, to be honest, and not to disrupt business.

Employees should carry out and follow orders of the employer as long as they are legal. They should work with reasonable care and skill, and look after the employer's property when using it.

Employees shall not compete in business against the employer while still working for them as an employee (conflict of interests should be declared). Employees are not to take bribes.

Can you be trusted to be a part that forms a whole (team)? Are you on a mission to support your CEO's vision? Are you clear of your company roles descriptions, goals and what is expected from you? If you are currently employed, count yourself blessed. If you are currently employed but report on duty for any other reasons than that listed on the obligations/duties that employees owe to their employer vice versa, you are more likely to become a liability to the organization, stealing oxygen from the business by incapacitating its productivity, your co-workers, and the organization's cash flow and for that matter it will suffocate.

No organization can survive when their employees are being unproductive, stealing from the organization, overspending, exhausting organization resources, creating a bad image for the organization and working unsafely.

Short lived Victory

Most organizations have short lived their victory due to slacking off syndrome. Their Management perception is, now that we have achieved our goals, production outputs are high and we are making profits, then we work less intensely than it is expected, and enjoy our perks during this period of little activity in business.

Management tends to wind down and their reporting teams spontaneously follow suit and that is exactly where all trouble begins.

When companies make a profit, is good. However, not all of the money should be spent on fat bonuses or on unnecessary spending and not thinking of the future. Until such time when challenges strike, that is when you see them running in circles.

High-performance organizations function well, even during recession time. They believe that it is possible to make a profit today when the economy is booming and as well in the future when there is a recession. They invest part of their revenue, have contingency plans in place and set aside provisions for rainy days. They perceive the economic downtime, as an opportunity for them. They efficiently utilize this phase to conduct proper inspections, rigorous safety audits, identify deficiencies, fix deviations, conduct maintenance and fix their equipment and machinery. They identify high-potential talent in order for them to sustain, be competitive and stay ahead in business. They further send their employees for advanced training and development.

Their points of discussions are more on safe work practices, continuous improvement plans, business continuity plans and structures. They are always in check of loopholes and do not wait for things to fall apart and start to wonder. They strive to implement the most efficient methods of working and to consistently correct the processes. It is crucial for organizations to develop a strategy map on how they are going to respond to economic downturns and how they can perform better in future than they did today.

CHAPTER 11

∞

IN RECESSION - GIVE THE KISS OF LIFE

However, who offer support to management when times are hard when it seems impossible to save organizations that are running at a loss, when there are production losses and everyone is pointing fingers at them.

There are still visionary leaders out there, who care about the future of their companies and its employees. Leaders who are values-driven. The psychological trauma is unbearable to them for not being able to save their employees' jobs and knowing very well the negative effect it will impose on their lives, families and the community at large. Who encourages management to carry on, who tells them that help is on the way, they are on the right track. Unlike employees, when Top management is indecisive situations, clearly they cannot turn to HR for grievances, against whom? On the other hand, go to the Labour unions or strike for that matter.

Blunders happened! So what? Are we going to attack each other, shut down our brains, roll over and die before our death? Let's all resuscitate life into each other. Attacking each other has never been a solution, and that is a trait of the weak-minded people. There is a solution to every problem. It only takes courage, teamwork and an action plan.

Tough times breed Great Leaders

Tough times breed great leaders they say. This is perceived to be the time where true leaders are being tested when there is a slump, not only when there is a boom, making profits and being celebrated. This is where the pillars and strategy implemented for your respective divisions or organizations will prove to stand the test of time. There were formulated for such a time like this. It's nothing personal. People will be frustrated and point fingers. However, you as a leader, you have to stand your ground and not be shaken by the noises. As a leader no matter what may come your way, you should operate on good business principles.

Never abandon or compromise your long-term principles that have sustained your organizations thus far. Even when operating under pressure, a good leader will exhume and display the level of strength from within and not the level of instability. A good leader will initiate, be innovative, improvise and bring change in a smart way. He will make an impact and bring benefits to the company.

Where do you draw Strength from?

It is crucial to know the source of your strength. It has to come from within. You have to condition your mind to be positive to develop a clear mindset and a shift in perspective and that will help one to make rational decisions. Assess the current situation and try to make sense out of it. Make it your new found reality, accept that it won't just go away, and go through it, by wisdom. Face the situation with contentment, have courage and integrity as a leader.

Remember, all that is happening now you have imagined it and thought of it before, hence your internal contingency plans and response plans. Now that time is here! It's inevitable. The enemy has arrived and is not smiling at you (low commodity prices, disengaged employees, producing poor quality products, loss of production, community unrest, exchange rate volatility, etc.).

Remember Noah, he built an ARK for the bad times ahead. When it flooded and there were rough winds everywhere, the ARK was swayed, tossed, pulled and pushed to every direction by the raging forces. Noah remained inside, he never ran away. He never blamed his fellow brethren who fall short from sin. Instead, he believed in what he has established. He believed the pillars that he made to build and hold the ARK together were so strong to prevail. He believed it was just a phase and that they will pull through this. Together with his people, inside, they formed a strong alliance and they prayed until it stopped. Suddenly, there was this calmness, sunshine, joy and everything was well and normal.

We need a Noah of our time. A leader in this era who would call emergency gatherings under one roof, involve everyone by conducting bottom up approaches as in this economic disorders everyone's ideas are valuable inputs to be assessed and test the theory. Rally brainstorming workshops, executing contingencies plans into action, have cross-functional teams to support the motion, offer support to operational teams and assign task teams to mobilize the recovery plan from disaster.

Leaders should not focus only on compensation policies, information systems, or training programs, e.g. as being a strategy. These are critically important choices, which should reinforce and support strategy, but they do not make up the strategy itself. The key is not in following a sequential process, but rather in achieving a robust, reinforced consistency among the elements of the strategy itself:

Arenas: where will we be active?

Vehicles: how will we get there?

Differentiators: how will we win in the marketplace? Staging: what will be our speed and sequence of moves?

Economic logic: how will we obtain our returns?

Better Operations in Action

Better operations in action ignite purpose, passion and foster growth and that yield transformed production line and supply chain entrenching a lean approach across the facilities and processes. Benefits of better operations in action are high-performance culture, sustained cost reduction, transforming to excellent production capability, cost-focused lean enterprise and strong supply chain partnerships.

CHAPTER 12

❧

BUSINESS RESILIENCE

Resilience is the ability of an organization to return to its original operational status after it has been impacted by a disruptive or disastrous event. To achieve resilience, you must first have the ability to perform business continuity (BCP).

Business continuity and Resiliency planning

Business continuity and resiliency planning is the process of creating systems of prevention and recovery to deal with potential threats to an organization.

Organizations need to have a set of contingencies, BCP wrote ahead of time by task teams appointed internally and other stakeholders. This will serve as precautions to be put in place to minimise potential harm to the organizations during adverse scenarios.

Lack of proper measures in place can cause organizations to face more challenges, incapacitate them to recover their normal business operations or end up closing down altogether. Labour strikes, community unrest, supply chain interruptions, loss of or damage to critical infrastructure (major machinery and equipment), are inevitable disasters or events that can negatively affect operations.

Possess the ability to recover from failure

In order for organizations to be successful, they need to possess the ability to recover from tough times and failure, withstand disruptive shocks and manage complexity. Resilient organizations possess these characteristics, acceptance of reality, a deep belief, reinforced by strongly held values, and an ability to improvise.

Resilient people and organizations face reality with staunchness, they take the pain and build something out of nothing, and they make meaning of hardship instead of crying out in despair, and improvise solutions from thin air.

Resilient Leaders

There is no formal education where leaders can build their resiliency skills. Life in general gives us many opportunities to continually develop coping skills and resilience. Strong leaders are very self-aware in general, and find ways to continue to build their resiliency skills. Through coaching, it can help leaders assess their ability to bounce back and adapt at work, and to continue to build the support needed to tackle the professional challenges faced in life.

Organizations can break resilience into four primary categories by maintaining physical wellbeing, direct mental perspective, fulfil life purpose while living your values and harness the power of connection.

■ Skills of Resilient Leaders

External awareness and appreciation of trends

We need leaders who can interpret long-term societal implications and anticipate how organizations are likely to react to them. These leaders must understand the risks and opportunities these trends will bring for their organizations, and they must be able to develop strategic options for the business.

Vision and strategy formulation

Resilient leaders effectively communicate the vision of what the organization is aspiring to become, how the organization will be profitable by addressing a societal need, internally and externally.

Risk awareness, assessment and management

Today's leaders need to address risks far beyond operational physical risks, such as risks to corporate reputation, stakeholder relations, business continuity or even customer demand. Leaders need to focus particular attention on high-impact, low-probability risks that could jeopardize the organizations' future.

Stakeholder engagement

To be truly effective at stakeholder engagement, leaders need to learn to be comfortable listening to and engaging with people of diverse backgrounds and points of view and see them as true co-owners of the business journey, not just a group of people to whom they are communicating.

Flexibility and adaptability to change

Resilient leaders demonstrate the ability to lead when considerable ambiguity exists about the best way forward. They listen carefully to voices inside and outside the organizations for new information that might require a change of direction, and they think creatively about new ways of doing things.

Ethics and Integrity

It is not enough to have ethics policies. Leaders need to show how ethics and integrity are embedded in the organizational culture and lastly integrating resilience into leadership development.

Through research, it was found that the organizations that invest in these competencies help create not only resilient leaders but also resilient organizations that support a resilient world.

Good leaders are resilient. They bounce back quicker from setbacks or adversity and keep the teams moving in the right direction, due to their capacity to make realistic plans, having self-confidence and a positive self-image, developing communication skills and the capacity to manage strong feelings and impulses.

Good leader see what is happening around them as an opportunity to learn, listen, predict and grow not to see a new market and societal realities as a threat, a time to retreat, and just do the same thing. All of these activities will contribute to improved physical health and greatly improved leaders' ability to motivate their team and produce higher quality work and they enjoy working with their leader again.

CHAPTER 13

❦

MANAGEMENT OPERATING SYSTEMS

The organizations' disciplines and processes should focus on management operating systems. This will help the business to strengthen its focus to drive long-term profitable growth, deliver positive outcomes and develop the business. Management operating systems will also enable organizations to execute their strategies effectively and can be later used for analysis when conducting their on-going assessment to keep the strategy in check.

Strategic planning

Management through the involvement of operational teams should tailor make their strategic planning to be satisfactorily realistic and attainable. That will enables management to think strategically and act operationally. It would further serve as a framework for decisions or for securing support/approval. It will provide a basis for more detailed planning and explains the business to others in order to inform, motivate, involve and assist benchmarking and performance monitoring. It would also stimulate change and become a building block for next plan.

Innovation and Technology

Top management should continuously encourage their employees to think, make decisions and implement original and new approaches. Management should strive to ensure that sufficient resources are available for innovations. Management should also be prepared to take the necessary risks to exploit innovation and growth opportunities in the market.

Successful organizations mostly achieve product line renewal at an unparalleled pace and made today's technological upgrades tomorrow's tools for maintaining their advances. It is the machine, equipment and devices that create and or deliver products and services. Process technology has a very significant effect on quality, speed, dependability, flexibility and costs. Utilization of all these three different types of process technology namely material processing technologies, information processing technology and customer processing technology is essential.

Customer excellence

Management should ensure that through finding and serving customers, they are where their customers need them to be. Through flexible and speedy responses to customer needs, product knowledge and capabilities to provide outstanding services to customers would be a key component of their success.

Supplier relationships

Suppliers make a vital contribution to the organizations' performance. Encourage suppliers to work openly and collaboratively with you to ensure you can continually improve your operations. Organizations should invest in modern IT solution to support the supply chain management functions, e.g. Electronic auctions, electronic requesting for quotes/proposals (RFQ).

Performance

Management should consistently ensure they deliver quality products and services on time and at record industry lead times. Maximize lean processing to achieve top-tier performance and the organizations' wide financial excellence.

Talent development system

Management should offer programs that enable their team to continuously grow and contribute to their success.

Operational excellence

Management should strive to be a production benchmark. They should plan and execute their plans with continuous improvements and innovations.

Through Ethics & Compliance

The code of business ethics and conduct should address the importance of fair dealing and compliance in all aspects of their business. They must emphasis on the concept of simply doing the right thing, all time. This will ensure that both Top management and the employees adhere to the code of business ethics and conduct.

Resource for success

Management should be committed to turning their organizations into "employer of choice." This requires looking inward organizations to ensure that the right people, with the right skills, at the right time and place, continually drive shareholders value and execute their strategy. Management should also strive to develop future leaders, attract and retain the best talent at all levels.

Corporate Sustainability

Organizations should take seriously their global commitment to sustainability. They should be committed to programs that ensure the health and safety of their employees, a diverse, engaged, and ethical workforce. Management should embark and have initiatives in place for development and enrichment of the communities where their employees live and work. That will definitely serve as a protection of the environment for future generations.

Organizations should focus on the elements of management like forecasting and planning. This can be accomplished by looking into the future to ensure that the objectives of the organizations are being met, long-term forecasting, predicting and adapt plans as circumstances change.

CONCLUSION

As we conclude this book, it is with great hope that each one of us will examine ourselves in light of business principles. Endeavour to be management, leadership and workforce that are empowered and determined to work smart, efficiently, improvise and strive to achieve remarkable outputs. The fourth industrial revolution is almost upon us and poses serious challenges for society and the business sectors. Therefore, the implications for education, advanced technology and skills development are significant.

In order for organizations to achieve their aimed targets, their organizational goals and objectives should be well aligned to their organizations' strategy and their employees aligned to the organizations' core values. It is of great importance to emphasize enough the need and benefits of an ongoing assessment of the organizations' strategy in every business sectors. Organizations should consistently conduct regular follow-ups to ensure that the execution is taking place as planned. Diligently seek input from employees at all levels throughout the various divisions and stakeholders of the company. Without frequent communication and feedback from employees, the business cannot adjust course when necessary. Continuous assessment and follow-up is essential to maintain a competitive advantage. Most importantly, Top management needs to ensure that their operational strategy is adjusted frequently in response to significant internal and external opportunities and threats.

Top management needs to reinforce and embark on achieving the benefit from the power of employees' engagement at all costs. Top management should continuously bear the responsibility to elevate and maintain high employees' morale by finding out what drives and motivates each employee to perform at a higher level.

Top management should remain focused on the core values. It is immensely important that they do their utmost best to come up with strategies, interventions, innovations and continuous improvements on their products, services or operations. This can be achieved by fostering a proactive approach to meet business objectives. This will enable organizations to reach their full potential to produce safely, profitably and ethically.

Organizations should put in place effective reporting lines, proper governance structures, operational excellence strategy and technology structures enabling them to consistently consider their values as a component of every business decision. The focus should be more on their commitment to empower and develop their employees, their culture in a safe and ethical environment. Top management should strive to foster the realisation of the positive effect of ethical values on transformational leadership and ethical climate in organizations. That to me sounds like a good turnaround strategy with an opportunity to enhance sustained cost reduction, improved productivity, operational innovations, maximizing human capital and commitment to business and economy sustainability.

SELF-ASSESSMENT

The purpose of this book would be greatly served, should at the end of the day, Management and Operational employees, satisfactorily answer the following self-assessment questions:

- Are you efficiently utilising all available resources and people, If not why, and how are you going to correct this going forth?

- Are you achieving and offering the best in class quality for all products and services and satisfying customer expectations, If not why, and how are you going to achieve that?

- Are you consistently correcting your methods of working and the processes, If not why, and how are you going to achieve that?

- What are you doing to invest in the future whilst you are performing well today?

Whilst at it, focus on people rather than profit!

The End.

REFERENCE

- Corporate annual reports and financial statement.

- Historical materials obtained directly from the companies, archive materials, historical documents such as prospectus, historical and current vision, values, mission statements, handbooks and journals and related developmental materials.

- Harvard and Stanford Business School case studies and industrial analysis.

- Interviews with Executive management, employees, former employees and external experts about the company or the industry.

- Labour Unions Journals.

- A practical guide to Labour Law, JV du Plessis-MA Fouche, sixth edition.

- Barney, J. (1991), "Firm resources and sustained competitive advantage", Journal of Management, Vol. 17 No. 1, pp. 99- 120.

- Chakravorti, B. (2004), "The new rules for bringing innovations to market", Harvard Business Review, Vol. 82 No. 3, pp. 58-67.

- Chimamanda Ngozi Adichie, The Danger of a Single Story

- Christian Hoehn/Taxi/Getty Images, By Susan M. Heathfield, Updated September 25, 2017.

- Creating Shared Value, Michael E. Porter and Mark R. Kramer.

- Daniel Pink, the Washington D.C.-based author of Drive: The Surprising Truth About What Motivates Us.

- Donald C. Hambrick and James W. Fredrickson, Executive Overview.

- Forrest B. Green (2006): Six – Sigma and the Revival of TQM, Total Quality Management & Business Excellence, 17:10, 1281- 1286.

- Harvard Business Review journals.

- Http/thesocialworkplace.com.

- http://smallbusiness.chron.com/rules-engagement-workplace-35325.html.

- http://www.trainingfolks.net/publications/pub_016/Delegation_2.html.

- http://www.upenn.edu/oacp/audit/audit101/operational-controls.html
- https://www.greenbiz.com/article/6-traits-define-resilient-business-leader
- https://www.thebalancecareers.com/top-mistakes-managers-make-managing-people-1917718
- https://www.wikihow.com/Keep-Chickens-from-Eating-Their-Own-Eggs.
- International Directory of Company Histories, Vol.68. St.
- James Press, 2005.
- International Journal of Business and Social Science Vol. 3 No. 11, June 2012.
- Larson, A & Gary, M, 2011, Case narrative of the Project Problems, Middlesex University, School of Computing Science, New York.
- Linda Hill, professor at Harvard Business School.
- Management: Leading & Collaborating in a Competitive World, Author Betaman / Shell 11th Edition, McGRAW-Hill.
- Managing People, Third Edition, Rosemary Thomson.
- Marissa Levin Founder and CEO, Successful Culture.
- Nigel Slack, Alistar Brandon-Jones & Robert Johnston, Operations Management, seventh edition.
- South African Journal of Business Management, Volume 36, Issue 2, Jun 2005, p. 19 - 26
- The Goal, Eliyahu M Goldratt and Jeff Cox.
- Why Work Sucks and How to Fix it by Cali Ressler, Jeff Gunther.

www.ingramcontent.com/pod-product-compliance
Lightning Source LLC
Chambersburg PA
CBHW071105210326
41519CB00020B/6170